Taintlessness

Omar Albeshr

Table of Contents

Love takes me captive; beauty binds my soul;
Pity and mercy with their gentle eyes
Wake in my heart a hope that cannot cheat.

Michelangelo

Introduction

Taintlessness is the noun of the word taintless, which is an adjective meaning free from or without taint; pure; innocent.

That is what I have always strived for my work to be. I've written most of the poems in this book when I was young. I wanted to publish this 20-years ago but never had the chance or time. So now this lifelong dream is, at last, a reality.

The Beginning

I've been here for days without end,
Confined in this tiny place.
A night wrapped inside a night, they all blend,
Being held captive in this embrace.

I hear an endless pounding hammering down,
I hear voices muffled by the gloomy surround.
I cry without sound; my face hurts when I frown,
I feel a weird movement all around.

Is my dull world falling apart?
Is this the end of my puzzling days?
Is gravity sucking away my rapid heart?
Or am I being pulled into a darker maze?

What is that out there?
A bright light fills my eyes,
What is that shinning flare?
This cannot be my demise.

My lungs suddenly are filled with air,
I scream with a riotous sound.
I am out, but, where am I? Where?
I open my eyes in this place, newfound.

To recognize her beats and her lovely voice,
I watch her silently admiring her tired face.
Feeling for the first time this sweet rejoice,
Through birth, I came back to my mother's embrace.

For Years

For years I have been lost
Within,
Buried so deep,
My mind and heart both tossed

Wishing for hope to seep

No sun rays tint my skin,
No moonlight rives my waves.
Only darkness sets therein,
Joy and glee as its slaves

My thoughts quiver,
They start to race
Think! Think! Grab tight those reins!
My soul flutters in its place,

Clink, clink, gripped by its chains.

My Life

My life's worth,
My mind's purge,
Under the surf,
My needless urge.

Poetry, above all,
To express and to enthrall.
The doors to my soul,
My imprints, my sole.

Nascence

This day shines once more,
With the first light of dawn,
The day rose with a thunderous roar,
Refusing to be just another day, foregone.

The sun torched the sky,
An imprint of its heat left behind.
The full moon protested and began to defy,
The whole universe refusing to vanish or retreat.

Celebrating an occasion of something great,
When I met my mother for the very first time.
When I started breathing since that date,
When I have known beauty that is sublime.

Such a jocund moment that overwhelms,
Such a magical day that is blazed into my reminiscence.
Seems very distant now, from different realms,
Yet so deep, it is immersed within my soul, ever since.

I Have Returned

I have returned,
My trip has adjourned.
Oh, how long I have yearned,
How much the longing burned.

Imprisoned by the foreign land,
Haunted more than I could withstand.
I run, but I find myself where I stand,
I crawl, but there are no marks on the sand.

I was chained,
I was strained,
I was drained,
I was in pain.

The misery had to end,
So my life could begin to mend.
My mind is no longer penned,
My heart sings, for joy is sensed.

My journey ends, I stop to roam,
I found my land; I needn't comb.
While all the roads lead to Rome,
My heart led me home.

Unnoticed

I'm timeless as time itself,
Standing against age, rage, and death.

Bearing witness to the ruins of anarchy,
Riveted with the old and new in harmony.

I've accomplished the invincible,
but can't you see,
I'm just a tree.

Welcome to the UAE

With open arms and smiles that rival our sun,
We welcome you with coffee, dates as sweet as our
embrace.
Our falcons soar as high as our pride that cannot be
undone,
With warm hearts, in our emirates, you'll always have a
place.

We lend our hands and nod our heads to all of our friends.
From all creeds, genders, and races, we live in unity.
Feel our sands that carry our dreams as we set new
trends,
For our future, our legacy, and community.

Gently Linger

Don't leave me to the night,
Gently linger.
Let your voice immerse my soul,
For a little longer.

Incarnations of my Love

Look no more, for I am here.
Here through the pleasant and the dire.
When it is murky and when it is clear,
During the cold, and amidst the blazing fire.
I am here.

I Hide

You ask me why I hide
Why I don't say what I deem
Why I go along with the tides
Why I keep to myself what I esteem

If I unveil myself to you
I'm afraid I'd be crushed with your censures
If I uncloak my thoughts for you
Your thoughts will be haunting my senses.

For all I am is a shadow
A meaningless being with a feeble soul
Human from outside, hollow from inside
With a minor role and a small goal

I always thought I was great
Always thought I was the best
But I never knew how much I'd regret
How I thought I was nothing like the rest

I filled my head with idols and dreams
I filled my eyes with beams and gleams
I didn't think dreams could die
I didn't know darkness would fill the sky

Emotions filling my heart
And life crushing my lungs
Emptiness filling my life

And life is just a bung

Life, I thought, will be a smooth ride
But here I am
From life, from you, and from everyone else
I hide

Stop Questioning

The blank page is blank no more,
Fury and despair have escaped through the door.
The feelings are touched at last,
You capture them and word them down so fast.
Life is as gentle as a silky cloth,
And love might be blinded with a honeyed scarf.
Hope is not a disease but a vigorous touch,
When you feel sad, it gets you out of that hutch.
They do see you when you are hurting,
But they try to help and relieve your burden.
They do stop; they will end, there is a sign,
Stop questioning, or life will pass you, and you will pine.

Take Control

Rules are made to be followed,
Yet, lives are there to be thrived.
You can't whimper and wallow,
No matter how much you've tried.

Seizing the moment,
Taking your chance.
Or living with the torment,
Not able to advance.

Make your own rules,
Live your own days.
Create your own tools,
Form your own rays.

Don't let life take control,
Live your dreams,
Follow your call,
Pursue your spark.

Chase the stars,
Befriend the moon.
Heal your scars,
Swirl your typhoon.

Know when to get in and when to quit,
When to hold and when to move.
When to stop and when to permit,

When to back off and when to prove it.

Wisdom is the key,
Success is the door.
Life is the sea,
Love is the shore.

Prognosis

This is my life that you presaged,
The pain and anguish you had signified.
But I thought it was just an imprudent forecast,
But it was true, and I was diminished with a blast.

Clueless as to how you achieve,
To know beforehand, the aching grief.
How you predict each tormenting throb,
So painful that I feel my heart will stop.

Have I been cursed by your evil eye?
That changed the mirth into a cry.
You stole my marrow, and I was petrified,
You added sorrow and left me mystified.

Have you bewitched me to lose my helm?
And be the ill-fated hero in this tragic film.
So that I live like the dead but at the utmost fear,
That you'll say a word, and death would be near.

I Mourn

Seas reluctantly threw their
arms to shores,
And the bees barely did their
branded chores.
Earth beseeched the sun not
to shed her light,
And dearly implored the moon
to keep out of sight.
You hear the howling sound of
the wind who still cries,
For our loss, she weeps to say
goodbye, this dire demise.
Even the trees were sad and threw
out their fancy leaves,
The impact broke our hearts, hence
the universe grieves.

Fragile Dreams

How do I rid myself of fear,
When every day I hear
My heart screams?
People live to hate, and nothing is clear,
Even a child's laugh, today, is not sincere,
So I hold on to my dreams before they disappear.

Birthday Bouquet

I wish upon you a very,
happy birthday,
To you, my friend, I give you
my bouquet.
But unlike these pleasing flowers in this array,
The love in my heart for you
will never decay.

Bashful Lover

You sit close to me
Yet
Your bashful eyes never
Fully return my gaze.
You yearn to look
But
Your brave heart suffers
Love in its early days.
Our hearts, since we've met
Changed in rhythm
and forever
Would fill our lives in mysterious ways.

Collision

I didn't mean this, nor did I intend,
To have these feelings
Of more than just a friend.
I fell in love; and in love, the rules tend to bend.
I didn't want to fool you anymore or pretend,
Something against my creed, which I won't defend.
Don't ask how this occurred for I, myself, don't
comprehend.
Where, how, or why this feeling began to blend,
All I know is that I don't want this to be our end.
I want us to forever be, and for our hearts to mend.

From this feeling, I can no longer hide,
I'm in love, being just a friend, I can't abide.
A feeling that cannot be separate from you or divide.
Denying my love felt as though my soul has lied.
Do you see how the grass greener on the other side?
Take your chances with me, let's go on a lifetime ride.
Without you, my world will collide.

Children of Aphrodite

I feel in awe,
When I look at the sky above.
Because I suddenly know,
That I'm incredibly in love.

I feel my heart is singing with rapture,
I feel my mind is dancing with joy.
I feel your love like a silky texture,
I feel your heart is astounding me with coy.

As if I was struck by Eros' darts,
I felt the yearning to hold you near.
I felt like love only exists in our hearts,
As if music only existed for our ears.

We are proof that love can exist,
From just a few glances.
That no one can deny or resist,
Falling in love and be lost in its senses.

Love is the sensation,
The everlasting force.
Love is the creation,
That feeds our hearts and souls.

Curve of Light

To stare sheer beauty in the eye,
Your perfect smile shines so bright.
I feel in awe, so much that I,
Will never forget your beautiful sight.

I peek through your soul,
When your eyes take me in.
I feel lost and lose control,
When your ray starts to fill me in.

Reborn in that sweet moment,
Revived by your heavenly beam.
Wrapped between the joy and torment,
If your heart, like mine, would only gleam.

Your brown fringe tickles your face,
As it waves and dances with the wind.
Oh, what lucky curls for they
Have felt her grace.

And that magical smile that dazzles the sky,
Made the moon and stars want to hide.
But they'd peek and pry; in the distant, they'd spy,
To find why your smile is so profound.

And the night lingers on and on,
Because the sun is shy to rise.
Unable to match your beautiful dawn,
She asks the clouds to be her guise.

Blush Angel

Blush, angel blush,
Let me see that pinkish hue.
When blood to your cheeks starts to rush,
I see, so clearly, the angel in you.

Your bashful eyes look away
And they stare blankly at the sea.
Trying to hide what they want to say,
'I'm shy; please stop starring at me.'

My eyes shifted,
My spirit sighed.
My mind drifted,
My tongue got tied.

In a whisper, only for you to hear,
I wanted to utter the words.
I wanted to tap the drum of your ear,
But I couldn't play my vocal cords.

Laced with Tears

In my own dim world,
I lie still,
In silence,
Only my heartbeats,
Echoing in my ears.
Overflowing thoughts,
Whirling,
As they spill,
Within my iris,
Grinding defeats,
Laced with tears.

Confessions

We talked,
for the very
first time
without
any separation.

It made
my feelings
begin to fly
as we
initiated
our conversation.

We walked
close by
with shivers
up our spines.

Even then,
I was dreading
saying goodbye.

I loved
so very
this precious
while.

How you

had sunk
all of my worries
with a smile.

And when
we both
have tried
to hold hands.

We swung
and brushed
our arms
in hopes
of reaching
the other side.

The touch
has made
my heart
decide.

That we
truly belong
in each other's
hearts.

You should know
that you make
me whole

You should know
that for you
I've begun to fall.

Because
I love you
from the depth
and breadth
of my soul.

For I love you
forever and more

Colors of My Soul

In a glimpse of your imagination,
Is where I want to be.
Wrapped in commemoration,
As if I'm all that your eyes can see.

You've brightened the dome of my sky,
You've given a meaning to my time.
The hands of heaven opened my eye,
And dazzled me with the scented thyme.

I pine for a moment with you,
My senses linger for your call.
My heart is melted within you,
Mixed with the colors of my soul.

Her Slave

I fell in love with the woman inside this girl,
Then I fell even harder for the girl inside this woman.
I had to look; to remove the shells to see the pearls.
To search inside and find the riches deeply hidden.
And I gaze upon her, as mortals behold the moon,
When she bestrides the dawdling nomadic clouds.
To glimpse the stark image of her face that is immune,
To time, age, or whatever life might wage upon us helpless
crowds.

She looks at me with those radiant eyes, and I am her
slave,
What sweeter prison would hold me as her featherlike
embrace?

Within these arms lies my home which my heart eternally
craves,
Such untouchable moments inhibit me, and with my soul,
they interlace.
In love, I was, even before my thoughtless senses,
celebrated it.
In love, my heart rejoiced, and in love, my being was
illuminated.
Identifying it made me stronger, it made me gain passion
and grit,
Nothing could derive my love, surely not this love,
impeccably fated.

Love What Are You

Love, O merciful tyrant,
O blessed sin.
Love, O screaming silent,
O blinding vision.

Madness mixed with sanity,
Chaos blended with serenity.
What are you? An entity?
Which you can fit inside a tiny heart,
Yet, you, larger than infinity.

O love, what are you?
You are inside my heart,
Yet I don't know,
How to define you.

Indescribable

I feel a rush beyond description,
I feel the heat of the new day.
I am finally living the fiction,
Where everything is going my way.

The sun is bright,
Clouds are dancing.
Our souls filled with light,
Our feelings are enhancing.

And at night,
Love overrules us all.
Beautifies every sight,
Lures us in with a musical call.

At night, our dreams come true,
Our visions become alive.
Our feelings would fit the hue,
And finally, our wishes would arrive.

I feel a rush beyond description,
I feel tender at my core.
I feel like I've cracked the encryption,
Of happiness, and its finally at my door.

Palm in Palm

Palm in palm,
As in heart in heart.
My head feels calm,
Because I know you'll never part.

A sweet endless embrace,
Between your hand and mine.
Fingers slowly touch and trace,
Each other's as they evolve and intertwine.

Oh When

Time, oh how merciless you are,
You bequeath me with this scar.
Oh Time, you cold-blooded czar,
You cast my cherished ones afar.

Lacking the wish to survive and remain
Shattering all hope of losing this pain.
Without a 'goodbye' I cannot explain,
How and when would I see you again?

Wanting to see, what could have been,
Life, with you, is an everlasting grin.
Life with you is to live, to breathe, to win,
But when would I see you again, oh, when?

Beloved Princess

I come with my courage; I come with my sword,
Yet, I'm just a common; I'm not a lord.
But I've rid thee of the demons I've slain,
I took away your nightmares; I took away your pain.
I ask nothing of gold or fame,
I only ask thee to surrender to this flame.

I've crossed all the lands, all the fields,
Yet I was stopped by your shields.
My heart you've mended, my heart you healed,
So it was bound to happen, in love I was, indeed,
So should you, my beloved, for love you have to yield.

Portrayal

I wish tonight, you had stayed,
Casting off the dimness of the shade.
Blasting off the nightmares that cascade,
For in my dreams, to you, I evade.

Because I love you,
I know I told you this before.
But I love you,
I've never loved you more.

Come to me, I don't want to be afraid,
I don't want you to leave; I don't want you to fade.
Hold me close, take my heart, and please invade,
My life, for I am, only through you, truly portrayed.

Consciousness Reef

With that looming gaze
That I often hated,
You look at me as if you
Know me so well.
I long for that answer,
Oh, so long I've waited,
How well you know me,
You do not tell.

How in vain, you are,
To think that you know better,
Full of dexterity, full of your
Own pompous inevitability.
Do not be tricked, oh please
Think before you even utter
A single word until the big
Picture glows in its own simplicity.

Then, speak all of your worries
And troubles away,
Let nothing restrain or hold your
Spirit back again.
And I'd listen, O very carefully
To what you have to say,
To have you as my guide
Towards the veiled virtuous lane.

To breathe that air of certainty,

The whiff of belief,
To feel adrenaline rush and
Be off to noble deeds.
Sensing your alter-ego being
Crushed against this reef.
As faith sinks your qualms
And you yield to its needs.

Safe

I pray for God in heaven,
That you and I are to be.
Above the skies, all seven,
And deeper than the mighty sea.

Come what may, we will prevail,
As these signs and reckoned.
We will not hasten nor fail,
Not even for a single second.

My ocean is gentle and calm,
No crushing wave will ever rave.
Let yourself drop in my arms,
And you'd be completely safe.

Just know what you mean to me,
Open your heart and listen.
I will surely make you see,
How true love has appropriately risen.

Out of Sight

Concealed by the clouds, are you able to respire?
Being in your full form, why do you need to retire?
Have we upset you, did we make you sad?
Did any of us, take away something you've had?
Please come out, let me see your beautiful face,
Break the lock of the clouds' embrace.
Come to us, light our sky, for we are blind,
Without you, our existence is redefined.

The Six Senses

I trace my dreams in the clouds,
I feel the breeze under my feet.
I spot the smiles amidst the crowds,
I see joy triumphs over the heat.

I hear the songs of pure delight,
I listen to the voice of generosity.
I converse with the wind late at night,
I whisper to entice the moon's curiosity.

I smell the scents of a sandy beach,
I sniff the aromas of passions' heat.
I adore how love can, sometimes, feel out of reach,
I love it, then, when suddenly we bow to its feet.

My Moon and I

My moon and I, we're in tune,
Fills my sky, brushes my dune.
My moon balances my moods and my tides,
When my moon appears, and when my moon hides.

Always around me, and within,
Even when my moon is cloaked, or thin,
But when my moon comes out in full sight,
In an ample form, there is no match for my delight.

With No Words

Hearts can speak without tongues,
Minds can talk with no dialect.
Eyes can chant beautiful songs,
Souls can converse yet remain silent.

Hands can touch from afar,
Mouths can taste the distant waterfalls.
Noses can smell the sigh of a star,
Ears can listen to the soundless calls.

To love with all your senses,
Yet it makes no sense at all.
This, that knows no boundaries or fences,
Got to you, and in love, it made you fall.

So strange yet so true,
Believing in something against your virtue.
Instead of finding love, love found you.

When you least expected it, love crept in,
With no words, still, the mayhem had to begin.
With no words, the magic has begun.
With no words, you found the perfect one.

Trance

For eons, she dreamt,
With an enchanting scent,
Filling her universe with jubilation,
A beautiful sense, free of lament.
With poems that cause an ascent,
To worlds full of love and infatuation.

Eyes full of gleam,
This is not just a dream,
Healing fumes saturate the atmosphere.
Thoughts run like a river's stream,
Ideas rise like a phoenix' steam,
Heart full of trust, soul drained of fear.

Tease

My sanity was long gone,
When you did to me what you have done.
From the first touch, I was a stunned,
When you do your thing, and then you run.
Your humor was out of this world,
Your voice is beyond strings and chords.
You hold my heart with your hand,
You make my whole soul, rise, and stand.
I look at you, totally lost within your eyes,
I ignored the dusk and the beauty of the sky.
I love you with the depth of all of the seas,
So be with me forever, and stop your tease.

Spirited Souls

Our spirited souls soar above the sky,
One-touch away from heaven, they underlie,
Against all logic, we stand strong, we defy
The whole world, no matter what it would imply.
We know we're mortals and our end draws nigh,
We are striving to be; we really do prepare and try.
We aim for the moon, the stars; we sure do aim high,
For no one can take our goals from our hearts, or ever
deny.

Legacy

Valiant warriors have long been dead,
But their fame has reached an end.
Poets' words are an everlasting mark,
From their existence and vigorous spark.

Bleak Future

The sky is filled with tears,
Heavy with the fumes of our sighs.
And the sun is clouded with fears,
Blemished, invisible to our puny eyes.

I envision my dreams within the shades,
And my thoughts cut into my mind like blades.
Until they clear the fog, only to find my dreams fade,
And the grim reality hit me as it begins to cascade.

Slowly the sanity begins to leak,
My dreams are killed without a shriek.
As I observe the massacre, unable to speak,
My so-called future begins, marked as: Bleak.

Falling Apart

Looking upon the moonlit oceans,
Hiding feelings, like my heartfelt notions.
Feeling my wounds, my hurting scars,
Losing my dreams and hurtling stars.

All that is left, this aching gush,
Nothing to agitate this breaking hush.
I speak without moving my lips,
I touch the shadows using my fingertip.

In complete darkness, I see you,
In obsolete dimness, I feel you.
Do you see these woeful skies?
Can you hear these doleful cries?

I can envision your extravagant grace,
Shining from your radiant face.
When I wake up, when I open my sleeping eyes,
I fall apart, and you hear my weeping sighs.

Hoax

Doth my love convey to thee contentment?
Or doth it confer thee containment?
Magic formerly, and promptly ensues resentment,
Purposelessness subsequent to fulfillment.

An amendment that was enforced upon us,
An apprehension that made thee flee, thus,
Vivaciousness distorted into complete bleakness,
Vigor has vanished, henceforth comes the epoch of
faintness.

Evil's ruse for unreserved obliteration,
Scattering mayhem, to expunge the population.
Enticing lovers of all breeds into predation,
The strong endures without commemoration.

Is this creditable for such sacrifice?
To lose oneself in such revolting guise.
Such decisiveness blinding your eyes,
Could be the reason for a grievous demise.

Despair

A blurred vision,
Because of my misty eyes.
Escaping their prison,
Leaving their confines.

Streaming down my cheeks,
Tears, those silver beads.
To meet my lips and then speaks,
Of pitiful heart of ache, it reeks.

I touch it with my tongue,
Feel its salty taste,
Of bitter life, left unsung,
Of dreams, misplaced.

Peace distort
Mirth drought.
Love forlorn,
Hearts are torn.

Losing my sense,
Losing my soul.
Bare without defense,
For others to hurt and control.

A title without name,
A sun without light or heat.
A field without rain,

A silent heart without a beat.

A night without day,
A being without breath.
A light without rays,
A life without death.

A poet without emotion,
A knight without a shield.
A travel without motion,
A kiss unsealed.

Heartbroken Soul

I love you with everything in me,
Every thought in my mind emits your name.
Your wind blows so strong within me,
I never thought anything could take you away, my dame.
I was left confused, despite your grounds,
I was left bruised, freeing all of my troubled sounds.

Even my daydreams ceased to console,
They joined my nightmares to haunt my soul.

What life is left to be lived? What fate is there?
To cling on the thin rope of hope.
How helpless my heart is, lying there so bare?
Waiting to be hung by the very same rope.

My tears got used to drenching my face,
My cheeks are never dry; my heart is never whole.
I drown in my bed, with only memories to embrace,
Nothing can bring back the smile to my heartbroken soul.

Illusions of Love

How can it be? In love, I was, and you were not.
How can it be? For love, I strived, and you did not.
You lied when you said you felt the butterflies I felt.
You lied when you said you felt the same love I felt.

You told me things that made me weak.
I should've known, of lies, you reek.
You told me things that made my heart jump.
I should've known that my heart, you'd stump.

You made me chase rainbows and dreams in the air.
You made me see you wherever I may stare.
You made me a fool when you deluded me.
You were so cruel when you eluded me.
You've clouded my thoughts of love and glee.
You've filled my head, so I wouldn't see.
Your masterpiece of illusions of love, before you run and
flee.

True Love is Yet to Come

I will not cry for you,
I knew you would not last.
I will forget that I knew you,
You will be part of my past.

I'm better off without you.
I'm saying goodbye.
I will not think about you,
Or my life will pass me by.

I'm wiping my tears away,
I'm waving goodbye.
Your feelings were just a lie,
But I'm strong, I for you I will not cry.

I'm putting a smile upon my face,
As I burry your memories.
With hopes filled with grace,
I'm holding on to my beliefs.

"True love is yet to come."

I'll Be Gone

When your eyes meet the moon,
When your ears seize a tune,
When amusing times ends so soon,
Remember me because I'll be gone.

When you feel the tint of a sunset ray,
When it becomes dark at the end of the day,
When you regain hope each time you pray,
Remember me, because I'll be gone.

When your hair dances with the wind,
When your life goes in a bitter trend,
When you go around and look for a friend,
Remember me, because I'll be gone.

When your hand plays with the rain,
When you fall in love and feel insane,
When you fall out of love and feel the pain,
Remember me, because I'll be gone.

When your heart melts as you hear a song,
When something feels right when its wrong,
When you feel every day like you have grown,
Remember me, because I'll be gone.

I Was Killed

The sun has set,
Light was choked to death.
My thoughts assailed by a threat,
That leaves my heart without a breath.

How could you leave the way you did?
How did you bear to see me cry?
Without a word to be said,
You went and left me to die.

Silence engulfed my soul,
Apart from the echoes of my heart breaking.
Forlorn in my own feelings, no one to console,
My heart amidst this forsaking.

I love you, though you are not here,
I miss you, but how would you ever know.
That you possess my whole being, my dear,
You lighten up my heart, and you make it glow.

Summoning up my fantasies, I live my dreams,
Fetching joy with such ease, my life shines and gleams.
How is it possible for all of this which you have filled
To fade away, when you left, and I was killed.

Misery

I always wonder how a beautiful thing,
Can cause my heart such a painful sting.
The feelings that she made me gain,
They shattered and were replaced by pain.

Since she found out that we fit,
She went ahead and limits she did set
So I can no longer hear, see or touch,
And this agony is just too much.

How she adores love was genuinely great,
But love turned to hate.
How she used to tear at a romantic scene,
Now, she would tear up the screen.

How changed she is now to me,
How very different she turned out to be.
To love and to hate, in a flash,
To live and to die, to create and crash.

So all that is left for me,
Is to cry, sob and moan.
Though misery loves company,
Alas, I pine alone.

Resurrection.

Resurrected, at last,
Rising from the tombs of the past.
Reborn, to stir up the long forgotten,
Revived to haunt the secrets within.

Think about all that you ever did,
Think about the words that you have said.
Torment is near, and so is anarchy,
Turning your wisdom into insanity.

Await the innovation that is coming ahead,
Attain the reality that it will embed.
Assure yourself of the cruel pain,
Amongst the joy of being utterly sane.

Days will drag on and on,
Demons will whisper until dawn.
Dreadful incidents will repetitively occur,
Drenching your body and your vision will blur.

Loved Me Not

Do not apologize; I need not hear you speak,
Your words are in disguise, lies, which I do not seek.
You have, entirely, broken me apart, you left me to rot,
You have deceived my simple heart; you loved me not.

Every dog has his day, and so you will perish and die
someday,
Only to be buried like a castaway, and your heart is left
astray.
Your soul will be haunted by grief, your voice muffled by
the sands,
Perpetual anguish with no relief; your heart resolves
nothing but strands.

I need not hear your voice; I have lost all that I desire,
No reason to rejoice, nothing to want, nothing to acquire.
I weep at this treason, and all you say that you did, is
mislead,
Unlike the rainfall, which has a season, my eyes forever
bleed.

A Young Heart

Oh, mystifying life, you astound me not with your ways.
How you define pleasure, and then wait for our praise,
The way you surge your wretchedness and mark our days.
Oh, pitiless life, do not expect me to gasp and be amazed.

You alter our lives as you wish, do you think of us as
slaves?
You command and order us until we are well in our graves.
In return, we watch our dreams washing out with the
waves,
We surrender to you and say sweet goodbyes to our
craves.

You give us no clues, yet we're supposed to follow your
trail,
We can see with our eyes, yet you speak to us in Braille.
What pain, what cruel torture you are about to unveil?
What sick satisfaction you get when we cry and wail?

Oh how feeble we are, oh life, we are frail,
We indulge ourselves, yet we cannot prevail.
In the sea of fate and destiny, we try to sail,
But between our legs, we drag a tail.

You try to explain, but I cannot comprehend,
You lay down the facts, but I do not see a trend.
That even though we'd all die eventually in the end,
Why did you take away from me, my precious friend?

To my friend who died on 2nd December 2003 at the age
of 23 years old.

Farewell

A confused soul,
A puzzled heart.
An unanswered call,
To be with, or to be without.

A triangle tilted,
Because an angle has lost its slope.
A pot with only two hearts melted,
Because the third has lost its hope.

Took his side,
Then be prepared for the pain.
You made up your mind,
Then you're set for heartbreak again.

And I will no longer be with or stay,
I refuse to be, for you, a number two.
And I wish upon you a happy day,
Because I will no longer be with you.

Scorned

I'm not like any other you'll ever know,
My heart is pure, and my word is untainted.
I am the white dove, not the ugly crow,
I am a beautiful artwork, which remains unpainted.

Extinction

The demons I've slain,
Have resurrected.
Beasts not stricken by pain,
Fierce and corrupted.

With vengeance in their eyes,
With fumes rising from their mouths.
Silencing the winds with their cries,
Soaring higher than my shaken doubts.

Drawn to the stench of death,
Attacking people and dead corps.
Torture set off from their breaths,
Shattering dreams, visions, and hopes.

I was destined to die and vanish,
Yet a weird sensation came over me.
So I got up and began to ravish,
The beasts and demons that I could see.

With my sword tight in my hand,
And with my faith clinched into my heart,
I began to strike, beat, and heavily land
The creatures, for their extinctions, are about to start.

My Dawn

How can I shut my eyes?
When tomorrow I'll be in your arms.
How can I sleep a wink?
When tomorrow, my heart will leap and clink.

How can I stop thinking and pondering?
When my mind keeps on wandering.
Thinking about what I'd say and what I'd do,
When tomorrow, at last, I'll be facing you.

Would I tremble and stutter
When my heart begins to flutter?
Would I know what to say or what to utter?
Being physically next to my significant other.

Would I meet your projection?
Would you know the depth of my affection?
That you're my reason for seeking perfection,
That through you, I view the world's reflection.

Would I be able to gaze into your eyes?
Seeking to obtain your silent replies.
Would you know that you're my sunrise?
And when you set, my soul dies.

So until tomorrow, I shall lie awake,
Counting the seconds until my dawn will break.

A Drop in the Sea

Standing under the heavy rain,
The drops collapse to the ground.
Yet tasting salty, Is it not mundane?
Mixed with tears that fell when I found...

That I was an irrelevant part of your vast world,
That I was as special, to you, as a drop in the sea.
That you played with me until you were bored,
And that I was too naïve, immature, and blind to see...

That my spell was fake and my sword was made of glass,
And like my hopes and desires, they shattered at last.
Realizing the truth that was cloaked with lies,
The lies, which I had to memorize.

Imprints of you and your love are in my soul,
Thoughts are streaming without halt, without stall.
But you came, and you've ended it after all,
I haven't forgotten you, I still recall...
You, but to you, I've already begun to pall.

Tenderness

She's waiting, can't you see?
That love possesses her soul.
So why don't you go there and be;
Her friend, her lover, and her all.

Tenderness is what she needs,
At times when sadness overcomes.
To collect the fallen beads,
When tragedy rolls its drums.

Drifting

I love my dame,
My dame loves me.
I burn with the heat of her flame.

Every day I strive to tame,
The beasts of desire in me.
I drive them out when I raid and maim.

Fills my heart with feelings without name,
Like rainbows fading in the sea.
The night overthrows me with guilt and shame.

Suddenly there's no meaning, all the same,
You, drifting distant, away from me.
Like a beautiful whirling star that missed its aim.

I find myself helplessly inside this frame
For everybody to glare at, everyone to see.
After you've left, standing alone and no one to blame.

Destiny

Destiny is not shaped by the hands of men,
Standing still, as the glow of their right is being dimmed.
Indulging themselves in an unbroken sin,
Yet, hoping that triumph, one day, will come to them.

Enough

Eyes ablaze, inflamed with lava dripping on my battered
face.
My heart erupted, blood sealing my vision; my abuser
remains unseen.
I've given all my life to make you smile, and this is my
reward.
This is the dark side of you, my love, but I can't take it
anymore.

Loneliness

Amidst the lonely folds,
My eyes are wet,
And my heart is cold.
My hands are stretched,
For you to hold.

But you are not around,
Thus, I search and look.
You're not here,
Nowhere to be found,
Hatred doesn't become fear,
It turns to despair that pounds,
That you will never ever be near.

My Heart

Why are you beating this hard?
I asked my heart.
For you're just a lump in a silly Bard,
You think your luck will change for such a rant?

Why are you beating so fast?
I asked my heart.
Have you forgotten the past?
The cruel pain that ripped you apart.

Think of the gloomy hours,
That you thumped alone.
Think of the shrivels and cowers,
Rapt between your cry and your moan.

Caged in bones, yet you're free in mind,
Completely alone, yet with others, you bind.
Filled with blood, yet you're not revived,
Shamed with dirt, yet you have your pride.

Think of the nights, dark and gray,
Think of your dreams, victim, and prey.
And one day you'll turn to stone or clay,
And the moment will come when I will die, one day.

Saying I Love You

Do you hear my voice across the lands?
Echoing my tone through this rhyme.
Beyond frequencies and their bands,
Saying I love you until the end of time.

Reach Up

I evade the grip of ghastly death,
I reach up for the bright blue sky.
I break away gasping for a single breath,
I shatter the grounds with my roaring cry.

The North Star

The North Star calls upon my soul,
I abandon my world, I leave it behind.
No burden confines me, no wall,
I leap to the heavens, existence redefined.

Untold Fairy Tale

A fairy tale untold,
A love story that was never meant to unfold.
A child that breathed his last too soon,
A day that never made it to noon.

Rotten Shame

My heart grows colder and colder,
My nightmares are getting bolder.
All the desolation of creation rests on my shoulders,
I writhed alone, but I wish I had told her.

That demons slithered within me,
And took nest in my chest.
I cower and hide, not wanting them to see,
How I wear this rotten shame like a crest.

Old Dream

The jagged road, long and uphill,
The burden that rests up here.
Within my heart, amid my core,
Resides an old dream.

The words that bash my head in,
The poems that awaken their muse,
Until the demons come and burn,
The last glimmer of hope and excuse.

As I Wait

As I wait upon Death's gaze,
I look at him and I stutter.
Chasing my petrified reflection,
Floating in his eyes,
I muster all the air within me,
And I wonder,
If I could even utter a single cry.
Alas, my last breath leaves me,
No cry, no whimper, just a quiver,
I perpetually fall and gently wither.

Death

Death is not the end of thee,
'Tis but the end of the beginning.
Ordained for all, none can flee,
'Til thy time comes forth ringing.

Thy heart ceases to invoke a beat,
Thy soul escapes breaking the chain.
Thy empty vessel has banished heat,
Never would thee be displeased again.

Thou art sleeping peacefully in thy grave,
Dread not what goes on above the ground.
Regret none of yearning, demand or crave,
Thou art parting to a place, more profound.

About The Author

Omar is an Emirati from Abu Dhabi. He holds a degree in Avionics Engineering, currently works in Tourism. Writing has always been a passion for him from a young age. In the late '90s, he began sharing his poetry on his website and online forums. He wrote under the aliases MalcomX & Taintlessness. In the early 2000's he was featured in Kul Al Ousra Magazine as a young talented poet and writer. He collaborated with many artists that needed words for their work and won a few awards. He collaborated with Mohammed Saeed Harib, the creator of FREEJ (aka Lammtara, at the time), who created artworks from his poems: "Unnoticed" and "True Love is Yet to Come". Omar has written more than 250 poems and has a couple of novels in the pipeline.

@ASRomar10
@ASRomar10